EAST COAST SAIL
Working Sail 1850-1970

Brigantine at Woodbridge c1900

EAST COAST SAIL

Working Sail 1850-1970

Robert Simper

David & Charles : Newton Abbot

TO MY CREW OF THREE

0 7153 5684 4

© ROBERT SIMPER   1972

Set in 11 on 13 point Baskerville
by W J Holman Limited Dawlish
and printed in Great Britain
by Straker Brothers Limited Whitstable
for David & Charles (Publishers) Limited
South Devon House   Newton Abbot   Devon

Contents

Introduction

To say that the camera cannot lie is placing too much faith in its ability, but old photographs are the most reliable source of information on the past. They are more trustworthy than the inaccuracies and myths which are sometimes created by artists and in some written accounts. Equally fascinating is the nostalgic quality of these pictorial records of the bygone days.

The aim of this book is to try and trace with photographs something of the activities of the working sailing vessels that were normally found between the North Foreland in Kent and King's Lynn in Norfolk. The great age of sail in coastal waters was from about 1860-1914, but on the east coast it lingered on for longer than anywhere else in the British Isles. The photographs will trace this slow decline right up until the sailing barge *Cambria* carried her last freight in the autumn of 1970.

The first men really to master the art of piloting the waters along England's south-eastern corner were the Nordic peoples from Denmark and North Germany. They came first as raiders and later as settlers. Finding a low lying coast pierced with estuaries, creeks and numerous shallow sandbanks offshore, the type of craft the Nordic people found most suitable were beamy, double ended, clinker built craft which required very little water to float. This type

Finnish three masted barque *Killoran* at Ipswich. When bound here in 1936 she was 120 days on passage from Port Germein, Australia to Falmouth with grain

The barge *Onward* at the Horse Ferry, Whitstable

of craft was widely used until the middle of the nineteenth century, indeed many of the beach boats still working from Suffolk and Norfolk fishing villages are simply modern versions of the Viking ships.

For cargo carrying the Viking type left a lot to be desired and gradually the larger cargo boats developed into a very different type of ship. These were beamy, round bowed vessels with deep draught and flat sterns which enabled them to ride out severe storms. However, their weaknesses were that they were slow and difficult to handle. When caught by an onshore gale they stood little chance of being able to beat away from the land.

The east coast mariner was very much a coastal seaman, accustomed to making use of the tides in the unpredictable North Sea and occasionally going as far as the Baltic or Iceland. Very seldom in records of ships owned in east coast ports are there any mentions of ships capable of making any profitable ocean voyages.

The exception is of course London which had a huge fleet of deep-sea merchant sailing vessels. London has always dominated the east coast, but after the middle of the nineteenth century its prosperity and rapidly expanding population created a bottomless market for every kind of product. From the Great Yarmouth fishing fleet tossing about in the North Sea, to the brick barges sailing under the shadow of the Kent Downs, all were organised so as to meet the requirements of this massive concentration of population.

The Londoners were keen on seafoods, especially when on holiday, and this demand created the final development of several local types of fishing craft. Since fishing is a highly competitive occupation it is not surprising that marine engines were adopted earlier than in the cargo vessels, although it is often forgotten that in small open boats, right up until the end of the age of sail, fishermen only sailed with fair winds; they maintained that it was quicker to row against the wind than to sail.

Steam vessels took a long while to make an impact on coastal shipping. Small steamers worked alongside sailing coasters from the mid-Victorian period onwards, but sailing vessels were able to meet this competition, particularly with smaller cargoes, and continued to be built and developed. The appearance of the internal combustion engine, however, led to a steady decline. In 1899 the sailing barge *Spinaway C* was launched at Ipswich with a small auxiliary engine, but the engine was removed two years later. By a strange twist of fate the *Spinaway C* was one of the last barges working under sail on the east coast, being in the Ipswich - London grain trade until 1959 and then was used for lightering until being sold as a yacht in 1967.

Finnish barque *Fred* being towed into Great Yarmouth.

Stumpie barges at Putney Bridge during the Great Freeze of 1882

Early failures did not put all ship owners off combustion engines completely. The London & Rochester Trading Co (now Crescent Shipping) had their first power craft in 1907. This was the steel sailing barge *Arctic* which had been built to win races in 1897, and as she was a complete failure a Dann engine was fitted and the sails removed. The Board of Trade in those days was quite happy for a barge to go anywhere in Europe under sail, but an engine was something novel, so the *Arctic* had to carry a small gaff mainsail 'merely to comply with the regulations'.

In the last days of sail traders the authorities changed their minds and distrusted anything which put to sea without an engine. It was the same with the seamen: at first they loathed power ships and considered them to be inferior. Later sailing barges were used by young coastal skippers as stepping stones up the promotion ladder. The ambitious seamen left sail as soon as they could gain command of a power craft. At the bitter end of the commercial sail era in Britain, when only a handful of sailing barges were left, young men who had grown up in a society where engines were accepted were drawn into sail, and were very eager to man the barges.

9

To begin with, power vessels could only be used in limited cases. The London & Rochester Trading Co, one of the largest and more progressive ship owners operated them in specialized trades. After the *Arctic* proved successful on a contract carrying beer from Battersea to Maidstone, the sailing barges *Atrato* and *Wyvenhoe* were motorised. These were shortly joined by *The Flame* which was actually constructed as a power craft for the London Motor Lighterage Co. However, in spite of motor craft existing, the London & Rochester Trading Co was still building wooden sailing barges at Quarry Yard, Strood for their own use. In fact the *Cabby,* 73-tons, launched in 1928 was the last full sized wooden barge ever built.

The construction of coastal sailing vessels had considerably slowed down by 1914 from the golden era twenty years earlier. In 1920 Vickers-Petter were advertising 10-450bhp engines for sale from their Ipswich works, suitable for 'barges, fishing boats and schooners'. That was the trend of the twenties. The remaining square riggers, schooners and ketches vanished from the seas or were cut down to motor ships with only steadying sails. Only the spritsail barges survived economically and even they declined in numbers as the twentieth century grew older.

Here we are attempting to capture just some of the atmosphere of commercial sail as recorded by numerous photographers. In plain black and white, only the image outline is caught. The tang of the sea, the screech of

Lowestoft trawlers being towed to sea. In the foreground is the *Acme*, built in 1895

Trading schooners at Woodbridge Tide Mill in about 1858

the wooden blocks as the little coasters made sail at the start of yet another voyage north after coal; this and much more of the feeling has gone. The age of coastal sail bloomed and died comparatively quickly. A man born in about 1895 entered a world where every coastal port was crammed with sailing vessels, yet seventy years later these everyday scenes had vanished for ever.

These photographs serve a dual purpose, for not only do they portray shipping, but something of the coastal regions before the mid-twentieth century development disturbed this peaceful area. Being an area of mostly low lying land there are few views of ports taken from hill tops. It is a pity, for such views would tell us more about a port than old maps. This coast line has certainly changed in the century we are examining; creeks and small ports have silted up and are still doing so and the sea has eroded away great sections of the coastline.

Not only the elements have brought about changes; with a rapidly increasing population the sea has been exploited for transport and sources of food. Harwich, the greatest natural harbour along this section, has been dredged considerably deeper, King's Lynn has been enlarged too. In 1867-9 the Alexandra Dock was constructed, as Lynn was the most suitable port for exporting coal from the Nottinghamshire and Derbyshire coalfields. While some old established ports have been expanded and newer ones like Lowestoft and Felixstowe have grown out of all recognition, others have faded away with the age of coastal sail.

These were chiefly the smaller ports which dealt with purely local trade. Wells is still accessible but its neighbouring havens of Blakeney, Cley and

11

Whitstable oyster dredgers

Brancaster have been given over almost entirely to pleasure boating. The least known of these North Norfolk harbours must have been Thornham. Small traders used to navigate the creek to its quay and warehouse, bringing coal and taking out corn. Coal and corn were about the most common freights of the sailing coaster on the east coast. Where there was no harbour, the craft were discharged on the beach. This happened at Bacton and Mundesley where goods for the North Walsham district were taken ashore. Even after the building of the North Walsham and Dilham Canal in 1835 many local merchants found it cheaper to land goods on the beach rather than have them brought by river and canal from Great Yarmouth.

Norwich must be one of the least known of Britain's inland ports. This beautiful city lies some eighteen miles from the sea and claims its right as a port, where from time immemorial ships delivered merchandise. Norwich port was in the king's hands, but this did not stop the growing town of Great Yarmouth trying to prevent goods going inland. In 1333 the King sent a stern warning to the Yarmouth Bailiffs about trying to force all ships to discharge there, instead of going on to Norwich. This battle went on for centuries, but in the period we are examining, Great Yarmouth had become the leading Norfolk port, although there was still traffic to Norwich.

Silting has been the greatest problem. In the Thames Estuary ports it can completely block up a berth in a few years, while from the River Deben right round to Brancaster there are dangerous entrances caused by the coastal tidal drift forming bars. The brave attempts to keep Southwold harbour

12

open are legendary. The Sole Bay men have for successive generations had to fight to keep the shingle from completely blocking the River Blythe. It is believed that the present site of the entrance was dug out after the same gales which dispersed the Spanish Armada in 1599 blocked the previous one. Over the centuries the amount of tidal water that has flowed out of the harbour has declined due to reclamation and silting, and this accentuates the problem.

Southwold fishermen turned to operating beach boats from in front of the town. This era is well recorded in the museum-like Sailor's Reading Room. The open fishing boats of Norfolk and Suffolk varied from place to place but were usually known as punts. Fishing from small open boats under sail was very hard; a Southwold fisherman told me how as a young man he had been out when most of the local punts had to run south of Orfordness for shelter. The fishermen finished up at Orford and spent several days living under sails thrown over the bows of the boats which were pulled up on the shore.

The Shingle Street fishermen devised a giant spoon for getting the coal out of ships wrecked on Orfordness. They gave up working boats from Bawdsey because they found that selling around the villages was not a wide enough market. These men lived in very isolated communities. They expected no help from outsiders and certainly rarely received any. This self reliant attitude sums up the age of sail.

In this book we are covering a wide area and a comparatively long spell of time. There are many gaps which I am well aware of but space is the limiting factor. The photographs which accompany this section are in themselves an introduction.

Finnish square riggers brought grain annually from Australia to Ipswich until World War II. Here the *Abraham Rydberg* is being towed down the River Orwell

The gun powder works at Oare in North Kent kept many barges employed. Here they are seen in Oare Creek in about 1925.

Coal was jumped out of the sailing coaster at most east coast ports. In 'the Jump' at Whitstable Harbour the two men jumped off backwards from the steps to raise a basket full of coal from the hold to the quay, and then the process was repeated to get the coal into the railway wagon. This was discontinued at Whitstable in about 1920.

14

Mud glorious mud. Every east coast river has acres of it and these vast expanses serve as a reservoir to help sweep the silt out of the main channel on every tide. Most estuaries are slowly silting up. In the old methods of producing cement and bricks, mud was an essential ingredient. Above, a gang with wooden mud-shovels are loading the barge *Eric* at Rainham, Kent. The difficulties of working up a creek with even a small barge were considerable and required local knowledge and hard work with 'setting booms'. The *Berwick* is seen in Conyer Creek; she was the last barge to load from Eastwoods brickfield at the head of the creek. This was during 1939.

There was tremendous barge traffic from the 1880s until the 1930s, carrying cement and bricks from the Kent creeks to London. Above, Portland Cement in hessian sacks is being loaded at the Smeed Dean, Murston factory at Milton Creek. The barge being loaded is the *Russell* and ahead of this is Covington's *Tam* of London. The Smeed Dean works are now derelict, but in their heyday they had about a hundred sailing barges. Most of them were built at their own yard beside the factory between 1870-1913 and they rebuilt their fleet between 1914-28.

The barge below is Smeed Dean's *Murston* at Burley's Dolphin Cement Works in 1907.

The number of Kent barges was staggering. There were 250 barges owned in Milton Creek until the mid-1920s. The creek is only about two miles long, running up to Sittingbourne, and the east bank was lined with wharves and docks which meant that up to sixty barges often left the creek on a single tide.

This shows some of Smeed Dean's barges at their Adelaide Dock brick works in about 1930. Above, the *Russell* is loading bricks. The group below includes *Histed* named after the village where the chalk came from, but originally called *Lydia*, and built at Ipswich in 1880. Alongside her is the *Argosy* with *Leslie* behind. The last sailing barge working from the creek was the *Dunstable*, trading until 1947.

MALDON VIEW FROM CHURCH TOWER

Maldon was typical of the barge ports, since it dried out at low tide. This panoramic view was taken on a town regatta day in mid-1890, the barges in the channel are spectator craft, the smacks appear to be getting ready to race, and the tiny fleet of duck punts is actually racing under sail! In the foreground the barge *Dawn* is seen under construction in James Cook's yard. Like Maldon's more productive builder Howard, Cook was building stacky barges for transporting hay, straw and timber. The Keebles had sold Cook the yard and ordered the barge *Dawn*, launched in 1897, for the local stacky trade. This was followed by *Lord Roberts* 1900 and *British King* 1901, all three of which are still afloat. The *Dawn* was purchased by Francis & Gilders in 1933 and 'Hobby' Keeble skippered her for over thirty years. The barge was fitted with an auxiliary engine in 1951 and was finally reduced to a Heybridge lighter. In 1964 Gordon Swift bought and rerigged her as a Maldon charter barge and later with her skipper, Barry Pearce, took over running Cook's yard.

18

The port of Maldon served much of central Essex and in 1677 a scheme was put forward to build a canal thirteen miles inland to Chelmsford. The idea was fought off by Maldon interests because it would have meant a loss of dues. However, in 1793 a navigation was opened which linked Chelmsford with the sea via a lock at Heybridge, on the River Blackwater below Maldon.

Most of the traffic in the privately owned Chelmer and Blackwater Navigation has always been timber, often discharged from ships anchored off Osea Island and taken inland by lighter. Some lighters were built at Maldon, but the timber merchant's normal custom was to use old sailing barges. In the mid-1950s the last Essex sailormen were purchased for such use from Francis & Gilders. The *Mirosa* was built by John Howard at Maldon in 1892 as the *Ready*. The name was changed in 1947, as Trinity House wanted the name *Ready*. As *Mirosa* she traded until 1955, and happily she was re-rigged as a yacht in 1964 and has since enjoyed a successful racing career.

There was very little trade into Brightlingsea, but many barges came on to the Hard to be repaired. The *Anglia*, built by Shrubsall at Ipswich in 1898 and then owned by George Ventris and Hibbs both of Brightlingsea, is seen being warped on to the Hard. The two other barges are the *Sirdar*, built 1898 and the *Victor*, built 1895. These were owned by Colchester oilmiller Owen Parry who sold the fleet to the London & Rochester Trading Co in 1932. *Sirdar* traded until 1955 after which they maintained her for racing. She is still afloat in 1971 and is kept as a kind of prestige craft.

20

Above is the Roman River branching off the River Colne and winding its way up to Fingringhoe Mill. With Snape, this was reckoned to be one of the most difficult places to take a loaded barge.

On the River Stour Mr S. W. Wrinch's barges used to load produce from his farms at Erwarton. Here in about 1930 is the tiny, tiller-steered *Cygnet*, built 1881, which mostly worked in Harwich Harbour taking wheat across to Felixstowe Dock. Also seen is the *Bluebell,* built 1888, leaving with a stack freight for London under skipper W. Harvey of Shotley. Before road transport, coastal barge traffic on the Essex and Suffolk coast was closely linked with agriculture.

Beaumont Quay was at the head of a maze of Essex creeks known as **Wal**-ton Backwaters. The *Mercy* is seen here in about 1910. As so often happens, there is a story behind the barge's name. Mr G. H. Dean, director of Smeed Dean was driving home in his horse and dog cart along Crown Quay Lane, Sittingbourne when the horse was frightened by a train and bolted. In the confusion the dog cart was tipped over and Mr Dean thought it was a mercy that he was not killed. His firm had a barge under construction at Murston and when she was launched in 1896 she was duly named the *Mercy*. This barge foundered off the Essex coast during a gale in 1918.

Green Bros Mill at Brantham, at the head of the River Stour had the little 90-ton coaster *Orion*, which worked with the Cranfield fleet. They altered the name to *Gold Belt*, after the Canadian wheat belt, because a shipping line wanted to use the name *Orion*. In 1939 the barge was laid up but was bought in early 1940 by John Corello who became skipper-owner.

During World War II she was a lucky barge, several times the wharves and sheds were bombed the night after she had left. On passage it was always the barge behind or in front that got mined. Once while anchored off Mersea Island on a moonlit night a lone German bomber circled round and dropped three bombs in a line to one side of the barge and then went round and did the same again. Having been missed twice, John Corello and his mate were very glad when the 'Jerry plane' flew off. It is probable that the plane was in fact aiming at the shadow of the barge's gear thrown across the water; they must have been surprised that they could not hit such a big ship!

Among a number of sailing barges in the Victorian period, the topsail schooner *English Rose* traded into Woodbridge and Orford. Discharging a freight was a laborious task at Ferry Dock, Woodbridge; a hand operated crane was used. At the Deben side farm wharves, or docks as they were usually called, it was done by hand. Such is the case with the tiller-steered barge on Waldringfield beach in the 1890s (below).

Woodbridge lost its position as a customs port in 1882, but there was considerable coastal traffic until the 1920s. The difficulties of crossing the bar at the River Deben entrance really killed the trade. Above, in the Ferry Dock are three types of sailing coasters. Nearest is the Sully's spritsail barge *Raybel* discharging barley for a nearby maltings. Built in 1920 at Sittingbourne, she is still trading as a motor barge. Behind her is a billyboy and the ketch barge *Ethel Edith*, 88ft, built in 1892 and traded until 1927. Her hulk is lying at Pin Mill with panelled stern cabin intact.

Some of the Scandinavian square riggers which brought timber to Lime Kiln Quay had to have part of their cargoes taken out at Kyson Point so that they could get up the shallow reaches. Barges however traded comparatively easily to Wilford Bridge and Melton Dock at the head of the river. Captain R. Skinner's 101ft boomie *Lord Alcester* which loaded 300 tons of coal and carried five hands traded with coal from the Tyne to Biscay ports and also traded fairly regularly to the jetty at Woodbridge.

The Suffolk estuary which winds its way up to Snape is called the Ore in its lower reaches, but at some indefinable spot above Orford it becomes the Alde. Some ten miles after leaving the sea its course goes back round to being within a few feet of the sea. This is just outside Aldeburgh and we see this narrow piece of land as it was in about 1900, before much of the hamlet of Slaughden had been eroded away. Today all these buildings have gone and only the sea defences stop the river and sea from meeting.

On the right the 'Three Mariners' inn has the sea coming right up to its walls and in about 1910 it was washed away. The smack, probably the *Ocean Wave*, in the centre is lying in Charlie Ward's dock and behind this is a ground-nut mill, Hunt's yard and, in the distance, the smacks laid up at Slaughden Quay. From medieval times ships sailed annually from Aldeburgh to the Icelandic cod fishery. The Victorian smacks were cutters or dandy rigged and were laid up in the summer. There was close association with Harwich in this cod fishing. The last smack to sail was the *Gypsy* in 1913, part owned in Aldeburgh and Harwich. She was probably also the last cod smack built at Slaughden, having been launched in 1882.

Snape Maltings at the top of the River Alde was the main shipping centre of this long Suffolk estuary. The barge is the *Dawn*, built 1890 and owned by Maurice Cowell, manager of the Maltings. In the summer the *Dawn* was chartered out for holiday trips. Most of the work to the Maltings was with imported barley for malting, a process which took place in the winter months.

It perhaps seems strange that the main import to Snape was grain, because East Anglia's main industry is agriculture based on cereal growing. However, this had meant that many ports and creeks had tide mills and maltings which sent their products to London. By the end of the nineteenth century many of the old mills had expanded to such an extent that imported cereals were needed. Few mills could handle a shipload at a time, even if they had suitable berths for deep-sea shipping. Therefore it was brought from the centre of distribution, London Docks, to the smaller ports, by barge.

Looking across Southwold Harbour in the 1850s the photographer has recorded a visiting Dutch botter and two East Coast luggers on the Walberswick shore. The scene below was probably posed in an accepted Victorian manner and is rather similar to the Waldringfield barge on page 24 where every man is at his proper station. Here on Aldeburgh beach are three Ipswich registered punts of a type found between Great Yarmouth and Walton-on-the-Naze. At one time, two Clacton fishmongers owned smacks which in fine weather anchored off the town.

Lowestoft is a man-made port created by joining Lake Lothing to the sea, as can be seen above. Shortly after, in 1844, Sir Samuel Morton Peto bought the harbour and developed it as a link with Europe. Fishing was a local industry which steadily expanded. The scene below shows just a few of the trawlers leaving the harbour in about 1900.

In spite of being an incredibly difficult place for a sailing vessel to enter, Great Yarmouth was the most important port between London and Hull. A fleet of tugs was based at Great Yarmouth mainly for towing sailing craft. Here the tug *Express* is towing the *GIC*, YH 193, the *Fashion*, YH 149 and the *John Macey*, YH 959 to sea at the start of the 1889 fishing season. However, with a fair wind and tide, craft like the Scottish two-masted luggers sailed out.

Timber from the Baltic was delivered by sailing ships right up to the 1930s. Here is the barquentine *Estonia*, 475 tons, built at Gutmannsbach in 1921; she was one of the smaller units of Gustaf Erikson's fleet. She was lost in October 1936 near Orskar, when on passage from Hernosand to Portsmouth. Her crew of eleven were picked up by a lifeboat.

The steel, three-masted motor schooner *Aar* of Hamburg, 330 tons, has frequently delivered freights to Great Yarmouth. Built in 1932, like most sailing vessels she is longer than the modern vessel of the same cargo-carrying capacity. In 1968 she was delayed in the River Colne, waiting for a spring tide so that she could reach Colchester.

32

Situated on the corner of East Anglia, Great Yarmouth was continually passed by vast fleets of sailing vessels. The Yarmouth Roads, the famous anchorage off the town, was not always a safe place. On Saturday 22 October 1910 the Norwegian barque *Ceres* was driven ashore on the North Beach, Great Yarmouth. Just forward of her mizzen can be seen a windmill pump, typical of the Scandinavian timber carrying ships.

A more typical scene for Great Yarmouth was the fish being landed.

Norwich is situated where several of the smaller rivers meet. Above is a view from Foundry Bridge of the River Wensum in about 1925. The boomie is probably waiting to be towed to sea, on the right is Everards' mulie *Scotia* built at Greenhithe in 1907. She was a contemporary of *Cambria* which Everards built the previous year. In 1965 while bound from Great Yarmouth to London with her last freight under the ownership of F. T. Everard & Sons Ltd, *Cambria* was caught by a gale and, after loosing her mainsail, finally made Dunkirk.

In the Broadland scene below, the Surlingham wherry *Meteor* is discharging coal, probably on the River Yare.

The topsail schooners *Commerce* and *Ellis* are shown here unloading coal on Cromer beach in 1877. The *Ellis*, 54 tons, was built at Hartlepool in 1858 and was owned by N. Newstead Field of Cromer for the first thirty years of her career. The beach trade was not without difficulties, for one autumn the *Ellis* was driven up the beach by a gale and spent the winter there. The following spring she was jacked up on to ways and launched into the sea again.

Because of her regular appearance the schooner became popular in the town where she was known as the *Plumper*. She landed the last cargo of coal at Cromer in 1887. The following year two Cromer men, W. S. Juniper and A. Blyth bought her and owned her for a further eight years before selling her to Hartlepool owners. The *Ellis* lasted until 1920 when she was wrecked at Jarrow Slake near Newcastle. Both these are typical of the tubby schooners used on the east coast before boomie barges were developed.

Cromer has never had a harbour, but like many coastal towns, once had a considerable maritime trade. The ships were brought ashore on the high tide and carts came out on to the beach at low tide and took off the cargo. In 1528 there were no less than thirty trading vessels owned in Cromer, and ship-owning on a small scale lasted until almost the end of the nineteenth century.

Below, the 61-ton topsail schooner *Commerce* is seen beaching with a cargo of coal in 1857. She has a stern anchor laid out ready for hauling her off the beach. Built at Stockton-on-Tees in 1846 the *Commerce* was first owned by Henry Sandford of Cromer who had previously owned another vessel of the same name. Later the *Commerce* passed to W. G. Sandford who still owned her when she was wrecked on the north Norfolk coast in 1876.

On the beach can be seen the double ended beach boats, of which the town then had around fifty; anchored off shore are some of the Cromer fishing luggers. In the 1870s most of these followed the East Anglian pattern of being converted to dandies.

Above is a view of Kings Lynn from West Lynn with the smack *Victor* in the foreground. Out in the main channel are a topsail schooner and a Dutch ketch. The port of Lynn is on the Great Ouse River and had strong links with Scandinavia going back to the times when it traded with the Norse settlements in Greenland. In medieval times cloth was exported to the Baltic ports from Lynn and in the nineteenth century timber was brought in. In 1870 Lynn had 122 trading vessels which employed 750 seamen. The counter stern smacks were landing about 100 tons of shrimps annually.

This is a view of the South Gates at Lynn in about 1905 with the ketch *Tiberias* of Lynn in the foreground.

Rigs

The wherry has a single gaff sail and double ended clinker hull and is unique to the East Anglian Broads. Being solely in inland trade it was an early victim to road transport. Below is a Norfolk idyll, a wherry in peaceful countryside. Both these photographs were taken before World War I. In the top photograph a wherry is becalmed on Breydon Water, the man appears to be wiping the sweat from his forehead.

A stumpy barge was spritsail rigged but did not have a topmast. It was the original rig used by the early nineteenth-century barges, which were literally sailing lighters. The stumpy was always the poor relation of the barge family. Built of rough hewn planks, the hulls were often well patched after the knocks received while drifting under the London bridges and in crowded docks. The gear and spars were often second hand and the crews' quarters were cramped. The hull shapes varied, some, like the *Admiral Blake* whose hull still lies rotting in Shepherd Creek on Deadman's Island, were swim headed like the London lighters. After the annual barge races were begun in 1863, barges and bargemen shook off the rough river image and became sea going craft manned by skilled seamen.

The *Rutland* is typical of the later stumpies in the Medway London trade. Her deck line is straight, without the shear that gave the Essex and Suffolk coasters such character. The stumpies were cheap to operate and provided ideal carriages for taking small freights up narrow creeks. Up to 70ft long, they loaded up to 80 tons (30,000 bricks) and discharged at places like Bow Creek, Regents and Surrey Canals and Brentford Dock. The *Rutland*, built in 1900, was one of Eastwoods County class. These brickmakers had sixty-nine barges between 1890-1940. The freights they carried caused the metropolis to spread over England's green fields at a relentless pace.

The river barges of this century had topmasts and set five sails. Because of these topmasts they were called topsail barges to begin with, but when stumpies started to die out after World War I, this rig gradually became known as a staysail barge. This distinguished them from barges which had bowsprits on which they set a jib.

The staysail was virtually always left white and not dressed reddy brown. It was very much a light weather sail as it put heavy strain on the topmast head. When racing, staysail barges frequently snapped their topmasts.

In this photograph taken about 1935 the Kent staysail barge *Rand*, built in 1898, has a deck cargo of timber. The mainsail and foresail have both been reefed to keep them clear of this stack. It was only for this kind of work that reef points were added to a barge's sails. Under stress of weather the sail area could be reduced without the laborious and dangerous operation of using reef points. On either side of the foredeck of the *Rand* are heavy sweeps. If the wind faded away the mate would go forward and guide the barge's drift on the tide with these huge oars. The skipper is peering anxiously from behind the timber stack.

Above is the round sterned Billyboy *Eva*; she was presumably one of the Humber ketch barges trading into the Thames barge area. The scene is the Bawdsey shore of the Deben entrance. From here, Landguard point and Shingle Street, shingle was loaded regularly as ballast.

The gaff cutter is the most English of all rigs as it was perfected by the Victorians both in work boats and yachts. Below is the King's Lynn pilot cutter no 1 as depicted by the local maritime artist George Laidman in 1907.

For coastal and near continental trade, barges were ketch rigged in the late nineteenth century. In official records they are described as ketch barges although bargemen always called them boomies. Some were fitted with square sails on the main mast and were sometimes referred to as schooner barges.

Above the *Eastern Belle* is leaving Sun Wharf, Woodbridge, probably bound north for another freight of coal. The lack of wind on this day meant that she drifted on the ebb tide until passing Ferry Dock, where the crew in a barges boat towed her with a line from the bowsprit end.

A particularly fine boomie was the *Record Reign* built by John Howard at Maldon in 1897. The 110ft long *Record Reign* is remembered as loading 320 tons and prior to 1914 set two square sails. Maldon was enormously proud of the 'Old' *Record*. She is reputed to have turned away from Maldon in a channel barely twice her length. On another occasion she is said to have left Maldon at mid day and the skipper telegraphed his arrival at Great Yarmouth at 6.30 pm. Fitted with an auxiliary in 1915 she appears to have been lost off Dungeness in 1926.

The boomy barges could not really compete with the steamers and small motor ships after World War I. Unlike the spritties they could not fall back into the east coast trade because they were not so handy in confined waters and often needed a tug to get them into berth.

Some like the *Davenport*, seen on the right at Rye in about 1935, had the boom removed and became a half sprit. However most of the boomies were converted to spritsail but kept the gaff mizzen. As the rig was a cross breed, it appropriately became called a mulie. This was the case with *Ena* which was built with *Thalatta* at Harwich in 1906, both were later converted to mulies. *Ena* was bought from the builders by R. & W. Paul and the X seen on her topsail is their emblem, said to have originated from the firm's early connection with windmills.

Every summer trippers arrived by railway at the resorts and part of the outing was a 'trip round the bay'. This poor man's yachting stimulated the building of special pleasure boats which made convenient work for the fishermen since their main fishing season was in the winter. The popular name for these boats was 'sixpenny sicker'.

The pleasure boats were yacht-like; above, the yawl and cutter are seen on Whitstable beach in about 1910. At Southend the bawleys took trips. Deck chairs were put down in the fish hold so that on breezy days the passengers all happily sat down below. These boats made a lasting impression on the Edwardian holidaymaker. I grew up hearing about a Felixstowe sixpenny sicker called *Moss Rose* and imagined she was quite sizeable but in fact a photograph revealed her to be only an open sloop of about 20ft.

Canns of Harwich later built special tripper boats for Southend. Clacton Pier had landing steps for the local pleasure boats which were similar to the Colne smacks only with open cockpits aft of the mast. The tremendous demand at Great Yarmouth evolved double-ended beach boats rigged as gaff sloops with a single Norfolk headsail on a bowsprit.

The oystermen of Whitstable went dredging in powerful sailing cutters like the one above. A similar dredger, still sailing as a yacht, is the 40ft *Stormy Petrel* built by Charles & Richard Perrins at Whitstable in 1910. Being regarded as a difficult yawl to sail the fishermen called her *Stormy Bull*. Annual races were keenly contested here, as at most east coast ports. The last one was sailed in 1936. Below, Whitstable yawls are jockeying at the start of an earlier event.

Fishing Industry under Sail

The autumn East Anglian herring fishery was a very ancient industry reaching back before recorded history. The method of catching the herring, like other fish which swim near the surface, was with a drift net. The vessels had literally to drift with the nets. Because the North Sea could build up short steep waves, the drifters had to survive very harsh conditions. Since the distance from Great Yarmouth to the main fishing ground around the Smith's Knoll was not very great, speed was not too important.

The medieval craft which went in search of herring were called busses, but by the eighteenth century, luggers were used and finally a type of craft evolved which was usually known as a dandy. This was the local term for a ketch rigged drifter.

The herring fishery was well established by medieval times and for centuries was monopolized first by the north German ports and then by Holland. There was great enmity between the Dutch and the English fishermen, but a custom grew up whereby the Dutch arrived every autumn at Great Yarmouth. This however had died out by about 1830, by which time the Scottish boats had begun following the herring every year. The autumn fishery was opened with a ceremony of 'wetting the nets' on the Sunday nearest Michaelmas when the fishermen received the blessing of the church on their labours. A Herring Fair was also held which in time gave way to a larger fair held on the South Denes.

The lives of people living in Great Yarmouth were largely dominated by the herring. Every year the numbers of drifters owned in the town increased and so did the numbers of boats which arrived from other fishing stations. The two-mile-long harbour from the bridge to the sea, which in fact is the sea outlet for three rivers, was packed with drifters landing their catch. It finally reached a peak in 1913 when 1,163 boats took part in the fishery. By this time steam had really superseded sail. World War I closed the European and Russian markets where eighty-seven per cent of the catch had been exported. A decline set in and the fishery finally died out in the mid-1960s.

Neither Great Yarmouth nor Lowestoft had trawlers before the middle of the nineteenth century when smacks from Barking, Ramsgate and Torbay came and their crews settled here. Being near the then rich North Sea grounds they soon became the prime fishing stations in Britain. The trawlers required a powerful rig to tow their beam trawls. Above are shown some Yarmouth cutters of about 1870 owned by Samuel Smith ('Old Coffee Smith') transferring their catch to the fastest cutter, which then raced to Billingsgate Market.

In about 1880 the cutters were replaced by ketches because of the difficulties of handling their huge booms at sea. Here the *Kemes*, LT 1086 is leaving Lowestoft; the crew have just run out the bowsprit.

The difference between Lowestoft drifters and trawlers shows up clearly in this view. On the left is the drifter *Shamrock*, built 1899 with the dandy rig, a short mast and generally less weight aloft to reduce rolling. The trawler *Citizen*, built 1893, has a more conventional ketch rig.

The Victorian habit of having shrimps for tea triggered off the development of inshore, day, shrimping boats. Although known as cutters by the men who sailed them, the Great Yarmouth shrimpers had only a single head-sail, probably copied from the Broads yachts. These shrimpers did not appear until about 1870; there were sixty-five boats in about 1900 and in 1931 only four of the thirty-one boats had no engines.

Sailing trawlers worked from Lowestoft until 1939. Some of the last ones were *Our Laddie*, *Our Merit*, *Our Need*, *Girl Edna*, *Telesia*, *Kestrel* and *Colinda*, which later, as a houseboat, sank in the River Deben. LT 1265 (above) is *Our Laddie*, entering the harbour under reefed sails, while *Our Merit* (below) is under full sail.

Most towns and villages along the east coast developed a type of fishing craft for purely local conditions. Along the north Norfolk coast, clinker-hulled double-ended boats were favoured by fishermen working off the beach. Some, like the Cromer crabboat *Boy John* YH 102, seen here (below) in 1901 with her owner William Cox launching her, had a simple lug sail.

For working in estuaries the fishermen preferred a gaff cutter. The smacks differed slightly in size and general appearance at each fishing village. Above a smack drifts down the River Deben off Waldringfield, one of Mason's barges is at the Cement Works quay.

The *Boadicea* CK 213 is an Essex oyster smack with a transom stern which was popular before the counter stern evolved. She was actually built in 1808 but when seen below with a beam trawl on her deck in the 1950s, she had been rebuilt several times. These smacks spent their working lives within sight of their home port.

A Colchester registered smack is seen on the right prepared for a strong blow. The mainsail is reefed and the storm 'spitfire' jib bent, but in the starboard rigging is a heavy sweep, handy for rowing in case of a calm.

Below is Alfa Pitt at Maldon on his smack *Skylark* which he worked single handed in the 1950s.

Above is part of a watercolour of Harwich Harbour in about 1810 show-
ing a peter boat. This type of boat was spritsail rigged and had a fish-well
amidships. Because this well divided the craft in half, the Medway fishermen
later called their boats 'dobles' a corruption of 'double boats'.

The peter boats of the Thames Estuary had, by the 1870s, developed into
bawleys, again a corrupted name, probably meaning a 'boiler boat'. The bawleys were all transom sterned which gave a wide beam so that the resulting
stability meant they did not spill water from their boilers while cooking the
shrimps on the way home. Many 36ft long bawleys had a 50ft mast from
deck to topmast truck. On the opposite page the Leigh bawley *Bona* is racing
in 1904 under a vast sail area. Built at Brightlingsea in 1903 by Aldous, this
bawley was ordered by 'Bona' Kirby who earned the capital for her as a
hand on the yacht *Bona*. The bawley *Bona* has recently been rebuilt.

Canns of Harwich built about thirty bawleys for Leigh, including the
famous prize winner *Doris*, and one for Harwich. Of the three other Harwich
builders, McLearon built for both Harwich and Leigh, C. Vincent built for
Leigh, and Norman Bros mainly for Harwich fishermen. In the Harwich
Borough Cup races before World War I, the winners were Norman Bros'
Moss Rose, *Wings of Morning*, Cann's *Irene*. J. Good's Vaux built *Auto
da Fe* won the cup outright.

The first Harwich boat to have an engine was Bert Good's *Who Would
Have Thought It* in 1919. This was a smack but the first bawley was the
Lilian. The last Harwich boat under sail only was E. & J. Smith's *LD & RI*
which worked up to 1939. Originally owned by Turnidges of Leigh, she was
given a boom in about 1930, a conversion that was called a boom rig by
fishermen. The Norman Bros built *Band of Hope* still sails as a yacht under
the boom rig and the *Auto da Fe* is being rebuilt.

Above, the Leigh bawleys are shrimping in amongst the Sea Reach shipping. Their mainsails are scandalised so that they move slowly over the ground. The bawleys' great draft was a disadvantage and contributed to their rapid decline. On the left the *Nil Disperandum* is shown at low water in Leigh Creek.

As we see above, Maldon in the 1930s still had a fleet of little cutter smacks. The *Skylark* and the *Joseph T* are seen below in about 1958, dredging oysters off Osea Island. The sails are scandalised, but they were also reefed because the sails were old. Built in 1901, the *Joseph T* was worked by the Claydon brothers until 1961 but a small engine had been fitted. Ernie Pitt's *Polly* was the last pure sailing smack working until 1956.

Because fishermen often worked from one port most of their lives, usually in the family smacks, every centre tended to have its own local, technical terms. The Whitstable oyster dredgers were cutter rigged, but were always called yawls. On both these pages are scenes of Whitstable yawls. The yawl 99F (*Faversham*) is doing some publicity work for the Royal Whitstable Oyster Co. These craft were big enough to do occasional freighting. The Seasalter & Ham Oyster Fishery Co sent their 46ft *Rosa & Ada* to Calais with oysters.

The largest Whitstable yawl was the ketch *Speedwell*, built for pleasure trips from Herne Bay, and which later worked thirteen dredges, seven men on one side and six on the other. The yawls were kept on exposed moorings off the town which dried out at low water. In an onshore gale they often lay on their moorings rolling water right across their decks.

Ship Building

The construction of wooden sailing vessels was a highly skilled craft. There were of course good and bad builders. Above is the launching of the *Olive May* from Wills & Packhams Yard at Sittingbourne in 1920. Although fitted with an engine when launched, she was the largest wooden spritsail barge ever built.

Between 1836 and 1921 well over 500 barges were built at Milton Creek. This ended in 1921 with the launching of *Phoenician* by Wills & Packham at Sittingbourne. A little further down the creek was the yard of Charles Burley who, like many Kent brick and cement manufacturers, built their own craft, often to provide work for the shipwrights in between maintaining the working barges. *Fanny Maria* is believed to have been built at Burley's Dolphin Cement workyard in 1864. Until recently her hulk still lay in the creek outside the sail loft. Eight barges were built here, including *Clara* of 1873 and *Charles Burley*, the last to be constructed, in 1902. The derelict yard has recently been reopened as a sailing barge museum.

Moving down the creek Smeed Dean were very prolific builders at Murston. The Burham Brick Cement & Lime Co also had barge building connections at Murston, but opened their own yard on the Upper Medway at Aylesford in 1873. The demand for cement and lime was almost unquenchable at this period, and the factories around Rochester Bridge were producing 10,000 tons of cement and lime a week and most of this was shipped out by barges. The Burham Brick, Cement and Lime Co had a cut dug up to Burham in 1878 and that year launched the *December* from a new yard there. Their own barge building ended in 1888 with the *Thursday* from Aylesford. Their fleet was named after the days of the week, the months and the four seasons, and all had large white Bco in their topsails.

Racing stimulated owners into experimenting with new hull shapes but most owners kept to the traditional hull as they could not afford to risk their hard earned capital in gambles. Many owners started as skippers, bought part shares and then a whole barge. In the 1900s Orvis of Ipswich reckoned to build a barge ready for sea for £750. These were the days when a new sprit cost £7 10s (£7.50) and a shipwright's wage was £1 7s (£1.35) a week. It all sounds cheap, but it needed a great deal of hard work and good managerial ability to step from skipper to owner as well. Many made it, although one Ipswich skipper-part-owner is supposed to have exercised such personal economies as drinking hot water and sugar to save paying for milk and tea.

F. W. Horlock was one of the men who started with a half share in a barge and developed into a ship owner. After World War I he turned to building barges almost as a hobby. Since wood was too expensive, Horlock's had a series of steel barges built at the Mistley yard, starting with *Repertor* in 1924. These were probably the only fast barges built of steel. In 1925 came *Portlight* which did well in the barge races. However, in the 1928 races Everard's barges carried off the prizes. Fred Horlock remarked that next year the Essex barges would be the winners, to which Everard only laughed. 'Alright,' Horlock said, 'laugh now, but next year I will give you a reminder.' And he did, for his new barge the *Reminder* was first in the Medway and Thames races the following year.

These Horlock steel barges carried a vast sail area. The original gear of the *Reminder* was massive, her sprit was longer than that of the *Will Everard*, a barge about 100 tons larger in loading capacity. This sail area was good for carrying off prizes on race day but for winter trading it was more than two men could handle and it had to be cut down.

The weakness of the steel barges was that, being narrower than the wooden ones, they were very tender. Once when I was on the *Xylonite* and we were sailing light on a blustery November day turning up the Thames, it felt as if a squall would push her right over. However, when I let go the topsail halliard she soon came up again. The compensation with a steel barge was that you knew that the hundred gallons in the fresh water tank was the only water aboard, while the wooden barges 'worked' and their crews had to do a generous amount of pumping.

Joseph Sadler had a sailmaker's business at Heybridge until he moved up to the lofts at Maldon next to Howards yard in about 1890. He is the gentleman with whiskers, watch chain and walking stick in the centre of this group. On the left is Bill Raven whose grandson John Raven is still a sailmaker at Taylors, on the right is one of the Keeble family and kneeling is Arthur Taylor who bought the business during World War I.

Fred Taylor succeeded his father and ran the business until he retired in 1969 when Mr G. Dennis took over. With J. O. Whitmore Ltd who served the Ipswich barges, Arthur Taylor & Sons have become the last place on the

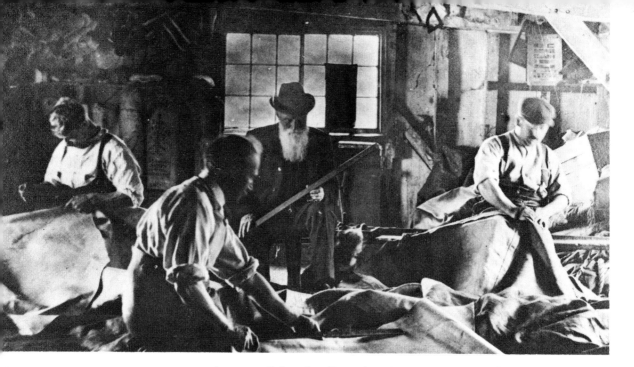

east coast where traditional sailmaking is carried out. The cut of a sail for working craft requires 'belly' to give driving power and is quite different from the sails of a modern yacht.

At one time all sails were hand sewn, but even with the introduction of machine sewing it is still a laborious and skilful craft; the average barge's mainsail requires about ninety man-hours to make it up. Properly dressed with red ochre and fish oils it can last for decades. In the 1960s the smack *Edith* still had a mainsail which was made for another smack in 1927.

The Leigh bawleymen used the cheapest canvas possible since the constant flapping wore them out quickly. Sometimes a special new suit was kept for racing. The Colchester dredgers had high peaked mainsails which made them sail closer to the wind. Some, like the French family's 33ft *Hyacinth*, had deck fittings for a topmast when built by Aldous in 1900 but a topsail was never carried. *Hyacinth* worked under sail until 1948 then under power until the mid 1960s. She has now been restored to her original sailing condition.

Every sail was individually made for each craft; however, Goldsmiths standardised their barge sail size so that they were interchangeable. Later the London & Rochester Trading Co did the same with their auxiliaries. The peak was cut higher to reduce the sail area and in the end they had about fourteen barges with the same sized sails.

The Strood bawleymen were particular about the cut of a jib. Len Wadhams remembers that on their *Minion* they had it cut low so that it dragged across the bowsprit which made the bawley faster. In 1924 the first engine was put in the *Minion* and over the next five years the rest of the Strood bawleys were motorised and the fishermen lost interest in sails.

62

Men and Their Ships

James Henry Fenteman (1855-1939) was the well known harbour master for the Milton Creek Conservancy for eighteen years during the period of the great development in the north Kent industries that used water born transport. Fenteman started as a boy working on a farm at Murston but had a longing to go to sea. He joined the Burham Cement Co's ketch barge *John Ward* trading to Rotterdam and his last voyage in her was to Ireland. This was done in very bad weather and took a month, but the return trip to London with a load of oats only took five days.

At twenty years old he became skipper of Mr George Smeed's barge the *Wave* but as there were two barges of that name in Milton Creek, Fenteman's was known as the little *Wave*. Later he became skipper and subsequently part owner of the barge *Yieldsted* until he came ashore in 1903.

This is Capt Frank George Webb at the wheel of his barge the *Mystery*, 73 tons. Born in 1876 Webb was an Ipswich man who obtained a master's ticket in deep sea sailing ships. He only went into sailing barges after he married the daughter of Joseph Hooker, skipper-owner of the *Mystery* and previous owner of the Ipswich registered *Lady of the Wave*.

Mystery had been built by Shrubsall at Sittingbourne in 1875 as a ketch barge for Robert Dodd. By the time Hooker bought the *Mystery* she was spritsail. In 1914 Webb and Jim Aldous, who kept the Ship Inn in the Back Hamlet area of Ipswich, purchased the barge from Hooker's widow. The barge was then skippered by Webb in the coastal trade and two years later he was able to buy Aldous out and become sole owner.

Before World War I started, Webb was trading between Ipswich and Strood and often took his wife and family along. Like many coastal seamen he always carried his dog on board and when he arrived at Ipswich he tucked a note in its collar and sent it home to let his wife know that he was on his way.

In 1916 while on passage across the Thames estuary in a gale one wang broke which caused the mainsail headrope to break and the sprit crashed down and snapped. With the sprit broken the barge was helpless and was driven across a minefield; she probably only survived because of her shallow draft. Eventually she was taken in tow and brought into the Thames. While a new sprit was being made up for her by Shrubsall at Grays, she lay in Tilbury Dock storing tea in chests for the government.

Once sailing again, *Mystery* started taking cargoes to Dunkirk and Gravelines; she also made several trips to Antwerp which involved sailing in narrow channels between minefields. Like all coasting spritsail barges, she was sailed three handed in those days; only when they became less profitable were they reduced to a crew of two.

In the photograph of *Mystery* on page 65 she is being towed into Great Yarmouth. This was a normal practice; the barges bound for Norwich were also towed there. Only the famous racing barge *Sara* is remembered as ever sailing to Norwich and it took her three days.

In 1921 *Mystery* got ashore on the sands off Margate and received considerable damage. After this she was virtually rebuilt; one of the changes was the old chain steering gear which was replaced by worm steering. The work cost about £1,000 which put the barge heavily in debt.

The following year Captain Webb, who was then 46 years old, struck a patch of bad health. His family were against him going back to sea, but he went and while on passage from Dunkirk to Faversham he collapsed with a stroke and died. The mate signalled to the coastguards of their Captain's death. Webb's terrier now stood guard over his body and would not let anyone near, not even the crew. When they finally anchored in the Thames the River Police had to come aboard and destroy the dog in order to reach Webb.

The family now had to sell the *Mystery* and she was bought by a Mr Last of Ipswich. She is remembered now as having spent much of her time lightering between Ipswich Docks and Butterman's Bay in the River Orwell. During World War II she lay on the mud at Pin Mill and in 1946 had the gear removed and was taken to Walton-on-the-Naze as a houseboat. Not quite her last passage because in 1971 the houseboats had to be removed and *Mystery* was towed to Melton by the *Convoy* whose acting mate on this trip was Colin Fox, grandson of Captain Webb.

The huffler played an intricate part in the coastal shipping scene. He acted as a pilot and extra hand when sailing craft were manoeuvred into creeks and harbours. Even the smallest creek had a local man whose knowledge of the channel made his services vital if the craft was to arrive safely at its destination. Even with a huffler a great deal of work and skill was entailed to get a sailing craft into a tight berth. At least one barge spent a week getting from Iken Church to Snape. The distance is only about two miles, but the channel is only slightly wider than the barge and they had a head wind, this meant that a kedge anchor had to be laid out and the barge dragged forward a short distance on the top of each tide.

Usually the huffler had been a bargeman or sailor and often had other employment. At Woodbridge the pilots had little smacks which they worked when no barges were coming. At Kingsferry Bridge, which links the Isle of Sheppey to Kent, there were six hufflers, one of whom in the 1930s was 'Doggy' Fletcher. He started as a mate on Wills & Packham's *Flora* until becoming skipper of Brice's *London Belle*. Later he became a skipper with Burley's, having their *Baltic* until about 1933, following this he became a Swale huffler. He is seen here as a huffler on the *Sidwell*. The *Berwick* on page 15 also has a huffler aboard. This ancient form of pilotage faded out early in the 1930s when small motor launches were used in most ports.

Passage Making

Passage making under sail required skill, patience and hard manual work. Given favourable conditions, sailing vessels could make a passage as fast as the power craft they were competing against. One thing a sailing vessel could never be was reliable, their dependence on the wind made the time taken to deliver a freight unpredictable.

However, taking into consideration the uncertainties, it is surprising how they remained working economically long after steam coasters were built. The account book of the Aldeburgh barge *Alde* shows that she was averaging, with fair regularity, two weeks on each freight. This was delivering cargoes, mostly from London to any port between Sandwich and Great Yarmouth. Smeed Dean's coasting barge *Youngarth* was trading down channel with cement in the 1920s and her passages were a little more unpredictable. Once she took seven weeks on passage from Milton Creek to Poole but her quickest freight was cement to Southampton and back within a week. Less fortunate was the boomie barge *Percy* seen here driven ashore on the Suffolk coast at Shingle Street.

During the summer months some owners used their barges for family cruising. Here the *Alde* is seen on a yachting cruise. Built in 1882 at Hunt's yard, Slaughden Quay for Thomas Adamson Riggs, she is believed to be the only barge ever built at Aldeburgh. Riggs owned the brick works here and the *Alde* and his other barge the *Exchange* took bricks to London and brought rag stone back from Maidstone to repair the Alde river walls. Her skipper was Captain Day of Dovercourt and the mate was George Brinkley of Orford. T. A. Riggs' son Walter became the owner of the *Alde* in about 1908.

Tragedy struck the *Alde* in 1913 when Walter Riggs' wife was drowned from the barge off Slaughden Quay. After this there were no more family cruises and the *Alde* was kept in the coastal trade. After being sold in 1916 the barge was damaged in a collision in the Thames and she finished up as a houseboat at Rye.

68

When there was a strong headwind coastal sailors were obliged to anchor in as sheltered a place as possible and lie 'windbound', until the weather improved. Even this had its difficulties. Here in the 1930s two sailing barges have been driven ashore near the entrance of Brightlingsea Creek. For many years Samuel West Ltd barges loaded ballast on St Osyth Beach, and on one occasion their barge, *Lady Gwynfred*, was blown ashore and washed into the municipal swimming baths near Bateman's Tower. Luckily the next tide was just as high and she sailed out again.

Not every passage was thwart with such harsh conditions; the Essex barges, below, are seen getting under way at dawn for a quick run down the Swin to the London River.

In this German photograph, the *Ethel Everard* with sails shot to ribbons is seen abandoned after the Dunkirk Evacuation of May 1940. She was later presumed destroyed by RAF bombing.

70

A cool winter's day in late 1956 and
the *Portlight* is running down the Wallet
off Clacton, bound for the buoys at
Woolwich. In the normal custom, she
would lie there until a freight was chartered back to an East Anglian port. As
the wind is aft, the mate has not had the
task of getting the bowsprit down to set
the jib.

This was one of *Portlight's* last passages under sail; she was cut down to a
motor barge not long afterwards. The
same is true of the *Xylonite*, built in
1926, another of Horlock's barges. Later
the same winter, skipper Peter Light is
seen, above, watching the *Portlight* one
foggy morning in the Lower Hope at the
Thames mouth. The author recalls a
great deal of work on the windlass that
day as we 'drudged' up the Thames.

It is a hazy September afternoon in 1955 and the 97ft *Will Everard* is on passage through the Wash to King's Lynn for another freight of Norfolk wheat. The diesel barrels and mainsheet in the centre of the horse give away the fact that she is under power. The last of the four big steel barges built at Great Yarmouth 1925-6, which included *Ethel Everard*, the *Will Everard* was to have one of the numerous adventures of her forty years as a coastal trader a few days after this grain charter finished.

Bound down Channel, the *Will* had her sails blown away while off Dungeness in a northerly gale. Next the 120hp Newbury engine broke down and the Dungeness lifeboat came out and took the crew off, leaving the barge adrift. The French trawler *Henri Jacques* tried to get the barge in tow, but the heavy seas swept the barge and trawler together with such force that the would-be salvage-craft sank. The French fishermen scrambled on the barge for safety and later another trawler the *Rose-Marie Robert* managed to tow the *Will* to Dieppe. After the salvage claim was met, she returned to Greenhithe for a refit.

On the east coast, sail lasted much longer than anywhere else in the British Isles, or for that matter in Northern Europe. Above, the *Portlight* with skipper Gordon Hardy at the wheel is seen on passage from London to Ipswich with fish meal in 1956.

When this photograph was taken there were only seventeen barges left working under sail and only nine of these were actually carrying freights on coastal passages. The remaining eight were owned by ICI and sailed under the flag of Woods of Gravesend. The PLA restrictions forbad explosive carrying by power craft. Wood's powder barges *Revival, Ardeer, Edith & Hilda, Ethel Ada, Gipping, Millie, Dreadnought* and *Asphodel* worked only in the lower reaches. Finally the ruling was altered and the fleet sold. *Asphodel* was bought by the Thames Barge Club. This club was formed in 1948 and, with *Spurgeon, Arrow, Asphodel* and now *Westmoreland* and *Pudge,* have helped keep alive the art of barge sailing.

Barging in the mid-1950s had a tremendous nostalgic quality; amongst most sailormen there was a real sense of comradeship. They were experiencing the very end of the era of working sail. There was a feeling that everything was being done for the very last time, which sadly was often true.

Barges frequently traded to the near Continental ports and very occasionally further afield. The ketch barge *Eastern Belle* (see page 43) went to Lisbon and another boomy, the *Blanche* fetched a freight of timber from Norway. However, the longest voyages under sail by flat bottomed ketchs were to South America.

Booker Bros of Liverpool wanted sugar brought down the shallow Demarara and Essequibo rivers in British Guiana to their steamers anchored off shore. The *Kindly Light, Clymping, Goldfinch* and *Leading Light* were sent. The rigging of the *Goldfinch* gave a lot of trouble during her voyage in 1930 so the *Leading Light*, seen above, was completely refitted at Par, Cornwall before sailing in 1933. Opposite, the *Leading Light* is seen leaving Par, and on passage in the mid-Atlantic.

Above are two views by Stan Hugill, bosun of *Leading Light* and *Goldfinch* on the Atlantic delivery passage. For this, firebricks were carried as ballast and the leeboards unshipped and stored in the hold. Built at Little-hampton in 1906 the *Leading Light* was one of the fine vessels built by J. & W. B. Harvey. Formerly builders of deep water ships, their barges were very much the 'schooner with the bottoms cut off' variety.

Passage making under sail was hard, but because it was such a challenge it gave a sense of achievement. In the days when coastal sail was thriving the crews also discharged the cargo, which was plain drudgery. 'Chubb' Horlock tells me that when he first went in barges as a boy of fifteen on the *Memory* the cargoes were still worked by hand. At places like Woodbridge Tide Mill he worked one winch handle and the mate the other when lifting 18st sacks. After 1923 'Chubb' skippered the *Vigilant*, often trading to Belgian ports. Calms were his biggest worry as they could not anchor in the North Sea and were in constant danger of being run down by steamers or drifting into lightships. Perhaps this hard seamanship helped towards Chubb's racing success. As skipper he has so far won thirty-six barge races.

Below is another barge connected with the numerous Horlocks of Mistley. This is the *Coronation* discharging coomb sacks at an Orwell quay at Ipswich in the 1930s. Built by Orvis at Ipswich in 1903, she was one of the founder barges of F. W. Horlock & Co and ended her trading days as a motor barge with the London & Rochester Trading Co.

London River

London has been the major centre of trade and administration in the British Isles since medieval times. By ancient custom the City of London had the control over the shipping on the Thames and they had the right to collect a levy on all goods landed. In order to collect their dues, the City compelled all merchant ships to discharge only at Legal Quays. In the case of larger ships, they lay at anchor in the Pool of London and the barges and lighters took their goods ashore to the City's quays.

In order to avoid paying the City's dues, carefully organised gangs specialised in landing goods after dark, usually bribing officials to look the other way first. In spite of smuggling, the City made large profits and naturally fought to safeguard their control over the river. In 1750 there was an Act forbidding small boats to go on the river after dark and the offence was punishable by fourteen years transportation.

The shipping on the Thames, however, steadily increased and delays and congestion almost brought the prime port of Britain to a standstill. If it was to survive something had to be done, so in 1796 a parliamentary committee investigated the situation and reported that the lack of dock space was serious. The remedy was to construct new enclosed docks east of the Tower. The realisation that London needed more quay space brought about the building of Londons dockland which was to continue throughout the nineteenth century.

The Saxons had made the first quay or hithe, but the early wet dock was at Blackwall and is mentioned by Pepys in 1661. Later the ten-acre Howland Dock was dug, which later became Greenland Dock and was absorbed into the Surrey Commercial Dock. It was the 1796 report, however, that led to the first enclosed wet dock with adequate warehousing in the modern sense of the word. It was completed in 1802 for the West India Company. By 1830 most ships were no longer discharged at anchor in the Thames, but went into the ever increasing wet docks. These were surrounded by high walls in an attempt to stop pilfering. At that time the Thames banks were still relatively green, but by 1880 the grimy dockland with squalid surroundings was general. It is a strange contrast that sailing ships, which are some of the most beautiful objects produced by civilisation should be so closely linked to some of the least attractive achievements on land.

The *W. H. Randall* was typical of the small barges that brought building material to the Thames wharves above the bridges, and to the small docks, and into the canal system. This barge, which has her topmast lowered was only 36 tons net and was built at Sittingbourne in 1876 for Will Randall. She was later bought by the Whitstable Shipping Co, and when this wound up in 1916, was passed to Daniels Bros.

In 1928 she was alongside a steamer at Greenwich with *Kathleen* and *Why Not* when the Cunard steamer *Virgilia* collided with them. In a sinking condition the *W. H. Randall* was towed ashore and later broken up.

Above is the little stumpie *Maud Hawthorn* at Fulham in about 1880. The rebuilding of Putney Bridge can be seen in the background.

Hundreds of small barges traded solely in the River Thames. Some of these like Burleys and Surridges barges, loaded 'rough stuff' (rubbish) at Lambeth Council Wharf opposite the Tate Gallery. Working above the bridges meant lowering the mast and 'drudging'; a term meaning controlling the barges drift by letting the anchor just touch the bottom.

A Bankside man called Jack Huggy claimed to be the last Thames huffler and was working in the 1930s. However, by then most barges were towed above the bridges. Allowing lighters to drift on the tide, controlled by lightermen with huge sweeps, was another normal practice then drawing to a close.

80

Below, the *Gladstone, Martin Luther* and an unidentified barge on the outside are lying at a brewery at the Chelsea end of Putney Bridge in about 1890.

The *Martin Luther* 41 reg tons was built at Murston in 1884 and was rebuilt there in 1910. These surroundings were typical of the kind of place cement was discharged. The Kent cement industry underwent a series of mergers, of which the final link-up in 1911 made the Associated Portland Cement Manufacturers the owners of the largest fleet of barges. They had at least 293; but in the 1920s these were rapidly disposed of. The *Martin Luther* was sold to Wesley Skinner of Woodbridge. During the inter-war years, the Skinners had five elderly barges working on the Suffolk coast. The *Martin Luther* finally ended up as a houseboat at Southwold.

Above is Pedlars Acre, site of the GLC County Hall, in 1906. On the left is the *Monica* built in the same year and owned by Miller of Battersea, who still had fourteen sailing barges in the general Thames trade in the 1930s. The *Monica* was still registered in the next decade.

Most of the six barges on Woolwich buoys seen above are Ipswichmen. On the outside is *British Empire,* owned by Francis & Gilders, which in 1954 caused a stir at Colchester by getting stuck under Hythe Bridge. She had to be pumped full of water to prevent her from rising on the tide and lifting the bridge off its supports. Because they were fairly central for the dock entrances Woolwich Buoys were the meeting place of all the 'seeking' barges. Here they lay waiting for orders and, since the bargemen were on a freight-share basis with owners, these were known as Starvation Buoys'.

Opposite below, the Ipswich barge *Venture* is seen in 1954 lowering her gear to go up under Tower Bridge; the Tower Bridge tug is coming alongside ready to take her in tow. Having arrived alongside Winchester Wharf, the wheat was shot down a canvas shoot. Loading the barge, however, would have taken four days. Opposite above shows the *Venture* loading grain at Winchester Wharf.

Above, the *May* is coming alongside a Silvertown Wharf in 1968 when Bob Wells was skipper. The 81ft *May* was built in 1891 by Cann of Harwich to trade to the Fisons Flour Mill, Ipswich. Her construction was supervised by Hastes who had shares in her. Arthur Haste skippered her for about thirty years.

Cranfields later had the *May* in the London-Ipswich grain trade, carrying 120 tons. Silvertown Services Lighterage Ltd bought her in 1964. They keep her for races and some 50 ton sugar freights from the Thames to the Isle of Wight; although by 1971 charter work had become her most successful activity.

On Sunday 23 August 1958, the *May* and the *Spinaway C*, skippered by John Fairbrother, are seen (opposite) leaving the King George V lock from the Victoria & Albert Dock bound for Ipswich. Cranfield's white moon emblem in their topsails probably originally came from Mason's Waldringfield cement barges. They had carried Cranfield's freights when returning from the Thames before the millers bought their barges, in about 1910.

Above is a tranquil scene in the Lower Thames in about 1951 with Everard's *Lady Maud* and *Sara* just making steerage way. Both barges have the distinctive Everard white painted transoms.

Survivors

Every age has its survivors which linger on after their contemporaries have gone. Below is the topsail schooner *Bernard Barton* alongside Lime Kiln Quay, Woodbridge, where she was built in 1840. She was one of some thirty-two similar schooners built here, ending with the *Ellen* in 1853. The *Bernard Barton* appears to be laid up, probably the boomie barges had taken away her trade. This deep draft schooner was sold to the westcountry and was cut in half and lengthened at Poole in 1862. Finally, as a Gloucester ketch, she sank near Lundy Island in 1899 on passage from Chichester to Cardiff with wheat.

Whitstable Harbour, opposite, was opened in 1832 and was the world's first rail-linked port. It was the last place on the east coast to have square rigged coasters. These were the colliers of the Whitstable Shipping Co which traded to the port until the firm was wound up in 1916.

Francis & Gilders *Mirosa*, skippered by Jimmy Lawrence, is seen near Tilbury Fort in about 1953 with a timber freight. This fleet of Colchester barges originated from a number bought up by Josh Francis after 1921, when the Essex agricultural trade was fading out. This firm was formed in 1933 and during the next decade they had fourteen craft. They began selling their sailing barges after World War II and the last of them, *Kitty, Centaur, George Smeed* and *Mirosa* went for lighters in June 1955.

Opposite is the *Veravia* in the River Orwell. Built as the *Alarm* at Sittingbourne in 1898 she was rebuilt by Horace P. Shrubsall at East Greenwich in 1926. She began trading between Remagen on the Rhine and the Thames. Even in the 1950s *Veravia* was trading to places like Goole and Guernsey. She was fitted with an auxiliary at Burnham-on-Crouch, after Nicholas Hardinge bought the barge in 1955. He was later part-owner of the *Venta* when she was sailed to Stockholm as a yacht in the mid-1960s.

Faversham is an attractive Kent creek port; here the *Ardwina* is seen in the early 1950s. Built at Ipswich in 1909, in the 1930s she had been a coasting barge owned by Goldsmith and was bought by Daniel Bros of Whitstable in 1951. Never fitted with an engine, she was sold out of trade in 1956 and was rerigged as a yacht in 1969.

The *Colonia* was the last barge trading under sail in the Medway area and was also owned by Daniel Bros. On the afternoon of 29 October 1956, she left the Thames bound for Faversham with bone meal. One of a sailing barge's weaknesses is that it makes poor progress against wind and tide, so that skipper Frank Bevan was forced to anchor that evening near Pollards Spit off the Isle of Sheppey. The wind increased to gale force and the *Colonia's* mainsail was blown away, and due to heavy rolling the barge started to leak badly. The crew of two sent up flares and the Southend lifeboat took them off. Some time later the barge capsized and sank.

Small motor boats took the place of hufflers at most ports. Above Daniel Bros's *Pretoria* is being towed away from Faversham with English wheat; she traded until 1954. Auxiliaries like Sully's *Scotsman* in the background would usually help the sailing barges. Sailing barge skippers always accepted a tow and indeed relied on this help at the end of the age of sail.

Barging at its best. Above, the *Venture* bound for the Thames in 1955 with skipper Mick Lungley at the wheel and the mate Pat Fisher coming on deck. Built in 1900 the *Venture* is now converted to a yacht, and is still practically in her trading state.

Below the wherry *Albion* is seen loaded with timber at Lowestoft Town Quay on 30 May 1950. The only carvel-built wherry, the *Albion* was built in 1898 as the *Plane*. She was restored in 1949 by the Norfolk Wherry Trust and traded for a few years. *Albion* still does some charter work. Her wooden hull has been treated with fungicides to preserve it.

The Thames sailing barges were the only British, sailing, working craft to survive World War II in any numbers. However, there were still several schooners and ketches operating as motor vessels around the west coast, while on the west coast of Ireland a few Galway and Aran hookers worked in the turf trade into the 1950s. There are the oyster boats of the Fal River which still operate under sail, but this is only for a few months of the year and is rather an artificial situation. The same could be said of the last years of barge trading; but until the middle of the 1950s there was still quite a fleet of barges 'seeking freights' and competing directly with power barges.

In her declining years the sailing barge was often not an attractive sight. Here is the *Durham* built in 1899 loading mud in Lower Halstow Creek in 1953 for the brickworks which was then working at the head of the creek. With the *Westmoreland*, the *Durham* had once been reckoned as being the fastest among the 'brickie' barges. Here her spritsail gear has been removed and the barge given a makeshift 'halfsprit' (standing gaff) rig.

The London–Ipswich grain trade was the last regular work available to any sailing barges. No seeking sailing barges could find enough freights to keep them working economically after the mid-1950s and none of the smaller fleet owners could afford to keep them going for sentiment. Thus Ipswich had the last fleet of pure sailing, working craft in northern Europe. The mill barge crews were paid on a weekly wage basis and to some extent the barges were warehouses. Their slowness in fact made them useful!

Even so they sometimes averaged a freight per week from the Royal Group of Docks, London; though the policy was to send roughly a barge a year to Lowestoft to be motorized. Above, in April 1954, six barges are locking in at Ipswich. These are the *Spinaway C, Felix, May, Ethel, Anglia* and *Marjorie*.

Cranfield Bros of Ipswich had fourteen barges at one time, and none of their fleet had an engine until after World War II. Another Ipswich owner, R & W Paul Ltd appear to have had twenty-two sailing barges at one time and about half a dozen small steamers. Both these owners seem to have bought up only the better barges, and because they carried perishable cargoes, kept them well maintained.

Pauls sold their last sailormen *Marjorie* and *Anglia* in 1960, having been disposing of their sailormen for over a decade. The *Wolsey* was sold for a yacht in the early 1950s and she is seen in the River Deben about to anchor off Ramsholt Dock on a yachting trip.

One of the saddest little episodes of the 1950s was what became known as the Sailing Barge Preservation Society. The idea was that a society should keep a barge trading under sail only. This, it seems, was born amongst the younger sailing-barge skippers and administered by enthusiasts. The publicity machinery rumbled into action and money was gathered, which resulted in the purchase of the *Memory*, 65 tons net. This bowsprit barge had been built by Cann at Harwich in 1904 and seemed the ideal choice. She had spent most of her career in the London–Ipswich trade and under Horlock's management continued in this type of work. There were often delays due to waiting for freights to an East Anglian port and sometimes due to a lack of a mate, but in the 1950s there was still fairly regular work available.

Then the *Memory* had a collision in the Thames and went on a yard at Grays where it was discovered that the hull contained more rot than had been previously realised. There was a plan to raise money to rebuild her, meanwhile the barge was laid up at Lower Halstow. Finally the barge was sold cheaply and the trust, with no money and no barge, collapsed. There was strong feeling for preserving working barges, but after this fiasco no one wanted to know about co-operative efforts.

When a barge could not get a 'pluck' from a motor ship, she had to sail. Below, the *Felix* is seen turning to windward, actually in Ipswich Dock, on her way from the lockgates to Cranfield's mills. *Felix* was sold for a motor barge not long after this. Cranfield's *Venture* was sold for a yacht in 1963, *May* was sold in the following year and finally the last of the Ipswich sailormen, *Spinaway C*, went in 1967. Although fully rigged she had been used for some time as a lighter and to take part in the races. Her present owner, Mr Walter Brice, keeps her at Hoo, Kent, and makes annual cruises to the Netherlands and occasionally to Denmark.

Officially after about 1930 there were three types of barges, sailing, auxiliary and motor. The bargemen however seldom used the term auxiliary as, if an engine was fitted, she was spoken of as a motor barge. There is a vast difference between a pure sailing barge and one fitted with even a low-power auxiliary. On the opposite page is Francis & Gilders auxiliary *Dawn* (seen being built on page 18) at East Mills, Colchester. The last sailing barge to poke her way up under the bridges to here was the *Mirosa*.

Above is another insight into how sailing barges managed to last so long. Here in the Wallet in 1954 the auxiliary barge *Tollesbury* is towing the *Marjorie* in usual barge fashion by having her lashed alongside. On this still, hazy day the *Marjorie* would have been weather bound at Ipswich, but instead she reached Woolwich.

The Swedish **galeas** *Solvig* was the first Baltic trader to be brought to the east coast for chartering. Built at Raa in 1926 his handsome ketch was brought over by Peter Light and started in the 1966 season. Previously he had the smack *Sallie,* built 1907. Above is the *Solvig,* based at West Mersea and seen here ashore for a scrub on Osea Island. Below is a deck view of the charter smack *Sallie* while racing in 1961. Following the local feeling for traditional craft, both of these have been kept as near as possible to their working appearance.

By the 1960s it was left to enthusiasts to keep barges sailing in any way they could find. The interest in the last traditional working craft created a strong, but purely local, feeling for them around the Thames Estuary. Barge and smack races were revived and, in 1963, a race for gaff rigged boats.

The annual races have greatly helped to keep sailing barges active. The race on the River Blackwater was restarted in 1962, and that autumn the first of a new series took place at Pin Mill. The traditional races were re-established at Southend in 1964 and on the Medway in 1965. Below, barges are seen in a Blackwater Sailing Barge Match passing Osea Island.

On the left is *Edith May*, regarded as the fastest barge left afloat, then *Pretoria* and *Arrow* both since reduced to hulks, *Maid of Connaught* now a houseboat and *Millie* which is still used as a cruising yacht barge. Even private owners cannot keep barges going for ever and every year a few more sadly drop out of the active list.

Charter work suits the few surviving traditional sailing craft in many ways. The accommodation is usually fairly unsophisticated, but no two vessels offer the same type of facilities. In order to keep barges sailing, enterprising owners have evolved their own systems. Mostly they are based on giving parties of young people inexpensive holidays in a friendly communal atmosphere, but the east coast charter work also caters for business conferences, film making and fishing trips.

Almost all the craft in the charter work are over fifty years old, and the short summer season suits them. But this short earning period gives barely enough to keep the vessels in good order. In fact, new gear and wages eat up most of the financial returns. The success of any venture depends largely on the skipper's ability to keep the charterers happy. It is the skipper who has the responsibility of the safety of the charter craft and this has to be the prime consideration. Here the *Centaur*, skippered by Tommy Baker, is seen first home in the Southend Sailing Barge Match with a charter party aboard. She was built in 1895, traded for sixty-five years and was then used as a lighter, before being rerigged in 1965. Since then she has been doing charter work from Maldon.

Above, the *Salcote Belle* can be seen from *Memory's* foredeck during the 1964 Pin Mill Barge Race. *Memory* was owned by Kemp & Beer Ltd, Maldon, and was doing normal charter work. This is very much a scene from the sixties. At that time no one worried how many passengers barges carried, but in 1966 two pleasure boats, one in the westcountry and one in Wales were tragically lost. Following this the Board of Trade began looking more closely at small craft round the coast. Now charter barges carry only twelve passengers and a crew of two. Everyone lends a hand working the barges. The Maldon charter barge *Kitty*, seen on the right, was rerigged in 1964 and has never had an engine. In 1971 she was still earning a living under sail. Built for the malt and cattle food trade in 1895 for Sullivan Horlock of Mistley, she was bought in 1938 by Francis & Gilders. Once, when Eddie Shrubsall was skipper, *Kitty* lost a stack of timber at sea. Another time, with a potash freight, she had her sails blown away and was rescued by the Southend lifeboat.

Above is the stern cabin of the *Cambria*. This layout was fairly standard in sailing barges, although *Cambria* is slightly larger because she is a coasting barge. Opposite below, she is seen on Pin Mill hard in 1967; certainly one of the most handsome barges built. The coal trade was the basis of coasting work until the early 1950s, but as coal became less used the *Cambria* traded more around the Thames estuary ports.

Above is the Pin Mill-based 89ft *Convoy* at Crown Quay, Sittingbourne. Like the *Cambria* she has high bulwarks of a coaster, called rails by bargemen, and lofty gear. Constructed of Sussex oak, the *Convoy* was launched at Rye in 1900. She was one of seven boomie barges operated by Crundall to bring Portland stone for the building of Dover Breakwater. Sold in 1907, she was a mulie until 1944. She was then converted to a twin screw motor barge in Wills & Packham's yard beside Crown Quay (see page 60) to help lay the Pluto line in the Normandy invasion. After the war she was returned to her owners R. Sully of London and for twenty years she was skippered by George Eastland, one of the toughest of the modern coasting men. The *Convoy* was sunk twice in Great Yarmouth harbour and finally run down in Tilbury Dock in 1968. Captain Richard Duke purchased her and completely restored and rerigged her.

There have been several survivors in this book, as indeed there must be, as it is a summing up of an era. Above is the *Cambria*, skipper-owner Bob Roberts, at Ipswich in the autumn of 1970 with cattle cake from Tilbury. This is believed to be her last freight before she was bought by the Maritime Trust. Below is the *May* still occasionally a trading auxiliary. She is just about to win the 1969 Blackwater Barge Race in this picture with 'Chubb' Horlock at the wheel.

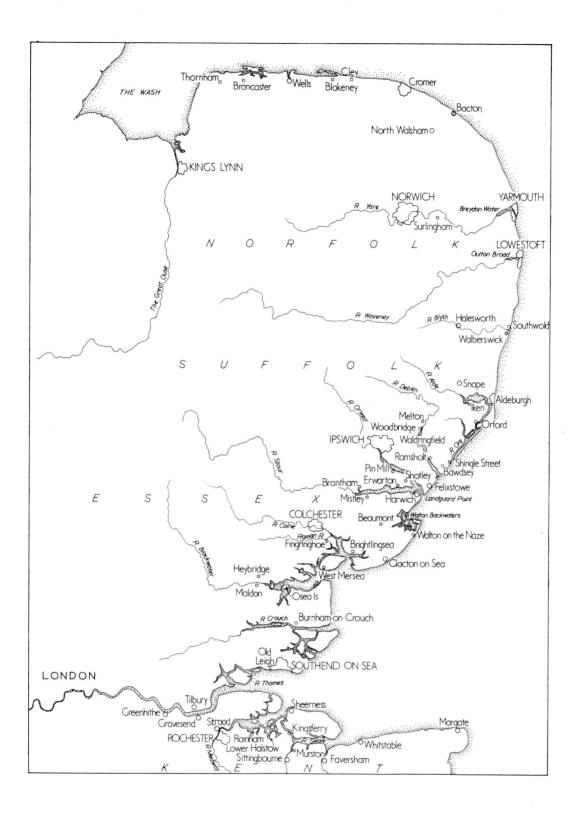

Acknowledgements

A book of this kind is not really possible without the generosity of others, and when such help comes from other writers who might have used the same material then that is real generosity. I have been fortunate in receiving this kind of help in some cases. Whenever possible I have tried to credit the holders of original negatives of these photographs but in many cases the originals have long since vanished. When several copies of the same photograph have survived, I have gone back as far as possible.

On sailing barge history I have received help from members of the Society for Spritsail Barge Research, notably Hugh Perks, T. Redshaw, Alan Cordell, Colin Fox and Roger Minter. As well as having lent photographs they have helped with identification. There are many old photographs but positively identifying them is a lengthy process. My own knowledge of the east coast has been considerably reinforced by articles in *Sea Breezes,* particularly by Bob Malster on Norfolk and the late Philip Kershaw's 'sail review', a regular feature that I have since taken on so that I can fully appreciate the work he did over many years.

Sincere thanks must go to those anonymous people on the staff of museums and libraries. They collect vast amounts of local history but it is often left to an outsider to bring it back to life. A little help in pointing in the right direction in research saves time. Mr J. W. Mitchley of the Port of Lowestoft Research Society has been very helpful, and so too has Mr Frank Hussey. His son Graham Hussey kindly lent photographs he took on barges in the 1950s. Suffolk is in debt to Mr Robert Pratt who before his retirement gave so much time to the Suffolk Photo Survey. Mr W. Bennett supplied facts from his lifetime spent in fishing from Harwich, particularly about bawleys. Help on Essex barges was given by Chubb Horlock, and the Medway by Tony Winter. Most of the photographs have been expertly copied by G. F. Cordy of Felixstowe. Space prevents me from mentioning the many more people that have helped. Without my wife Pearl's assistance this would probably never have been completed.

Sources of Illustrations

The figures refer to the page numbers; the letters a or b indicate whether the picture is at the top or bottom of the page.

Author's collection 25, 48b, 51a, 71a, b, 72a, b, 97, 104, 105a, b, 107a, b, 108a, b; F. Knights 6, 13, 77; Douglas West 7, 12, 14b, 45, 46a, b, 58a, b, 59, 89a, b; C. R. Temple 8, 31, 32; Ipswich Museum 11; Ford Jenkins 10, 29b, 49a; Alan Cordell 15a, 16a, b, 17a, b, 60, 63, 66, 95; Faversham Society 14a; Walter Cook & Son 18; Arthur Bennett 15b, 40, 41; Eric Boesch 19; Douglas Went 20a, b, 21a, 52b, 53a, 69a, b; Frank Hussey 54, 57a, 90; Capt W. H. Kennett 22; Colin Fox 23, 64, 65; Suffolk Photo Survey 24a, b, 27, 28a, 42b, 43, 52a, 67, 88; Aldeburgh Borough Council 26; P. A. Vicary 30a, 35, 36, 51b; Yarmouth Central Library 30b, 33a, b, 49; Port of Lowestoft Research Society 50a, b, 94b; J. L. Bowen 44a; Jack Hickish Collection 48a; Janet Harker 53b, 57b, 102b; Arthur G. Taylor & Son 62; Tom Riggs 68; Lawrence A. Mahoney 83, 85, 87, 98, 100, 106; F. T. Everard & Sons Ltd 70; Graham Hussey 73, 84a, b, 91, 92, 94a, 96, 99, 101; Stan Hugill 74a, b, 75, 76a, b; Mrs Molly Kennell 1, 28b; Steven Swan (originals from glass plates by A. Paget) 55, 56a, b; Norwich Central Library 34a, b, 39a, b; Greater London Council 82a, b; E. P. Olney 9, 79, 80, 81; C. Beagley 86; R. Dadson 93; East Englian Daily Times 103; N. Hardinge 102a; King's Lynn Museum 37, 38, 42a; William Wrinch 21b; Hugh Perks 44b; G. F. Cordy 29a.

Books for Further Reading

Sailing craft are now a very popular subject, but some books stand the test of time better than others. Of the numerous books about sailing barges, the ones which appear to be most read and are regarded by bargemen as being the most accurate are Frank Carr's classic *Sailing Barges*, Hervey Benham's *Down Tops'l* and F. S. Cooper's *Handbook of Sailing Barges*. All very different works covering different angles.

The books by Edgar J. Marsh record many facts and the dedicated reader will glean much from these. David & Charles have provided a useful service in republishing the late Mr Marsh's earlier work, as well as *Inshore Craft of Britain Vol 1 & 2*. John Leather gives further insight into Essex maritime ways in *The Northseamen*, while Michael Bouquet's *South Eastern Sail* to be published shortly promises to be well worth buying.